BUILDING YOUR
ADJUNCT PLATFORM

UNDERSTANDING
the Industry of
Academia

LANDING
Your First Adjunct
Instructor Position

KEEPING
Your Adjunct
Instructor Position

Michelle Post, PhD

Dedications

For God and Larry, thank you.

CONTENTS

Preface

Why This Book—My Story

"Here's my story, sad by true..." Oh, wait! That's a song from Dion and the Belmonts. Honestly, my story is not sad, but it is true...*so why this book?* Because I have and am currently living as an adjunct instructor, and I definitely did not start my career to do that. I guess you can say I have teaching blood in me; my Grandmother was a schoolteacher, and I have always loved learning and helping others to learn what I know. The reality is, I have a passion for helping others, and adjunct teaching is a great avenue to fully apply that passion.

I was on the "life plan" when working on my bachelor's degree; it took approximately sixteen years from the time I graduated from high school to when I completed my bachelor's degree. I started and stopped a lot! Then I got serious when it came to my master's degree and I accomplished it in 2 years; followed by my doctorate degree 5 years later. I needed the master's because I wanted to teach online; I had fallen in love with the delivery system, as I worked through my own master's degree.

However, I soon discovered, if you didn't have teaching experience, you could not be hired; so I thought a doctoral degree would ensure that I would be hired. I was going to be an adjunct instructor, and my career goal was, and still is, to be a full-time online instructor. I say goal, for I have not yet reached that goal.

I completed my doctorate in education with a specialization in "teaching and training online" and thought to myself, "I will be able to 'land' any teaching position now that I have my doctorate." Sadly, *that was not the case*. Becoming an adjunct instructor, in my humble opinion, is not an easy one, for there are thousands of qualified individuals seeking to become an adjunct instructor, so the competition is fierce. I will say that a doctorate degree does provide more opportunities to be an adjunct instructor, for it grants more degrees and subjects that I can teach.

There are dozens of books on how to become an adjunct instructor and online instructor (see the resource list included in this book for many of these titles), *so why this book*? This book is different because it provides a real success story of someone who didn't know anything about being an adjunct instructor and became one. This book also provides a great list of resources throughout and at the end of the book, no other book I have read on becoming an adjunct instructor does that.

It should not surprise you that there are politics and protocols in becoming an adjunct instructor.

Two equally qualified instructors may vie for the same position and yet one consistently succeeds for no reason attributable to resume or experiences. I address the politics and protocols that do not appear on any application form—these are the critical variables that can make a significant difference in your hiring success.

Benefits You Will Receive From This Book

I believe the greatest benefits you will receive from this book are the compiled resources. I have tried to put in as many valuable resources as I could find on becoming an Adjunct Instructor. Additional benefits gained from this book are:

- 10,000 view of the industry of academia
- Useful suggestions on creating a teaching resume
- How to create an Adjunct Instructor Application Packet
- A list of great self-assessment tests to help you learn who you are
- Suggestions on how to create your own personal strategy for obtaining your first Adjunct Instructor position
- Suggestions on creating a personal learning network

You will be given a head start in the process of developing your career as an Adjunct Instructor, and hopefully the powerful insights I will share will make the path easier for you and enable you to work efficiently and effectively as you build your platform.

STEP 1

UNDERSTANDING
the Industry of Academia

What Is an Adjunct Instructor?

A good teacher is like a candle—
it consumes itself to light the way for others.
—Mustafa Kemal Atatürk

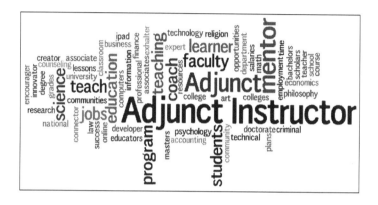

"An adjunct Instructor is a person who teaches on the college level but is not a full-time Instructor. Rather, an adjunct instructor works for an institution of higher learning on a part-time basis. They can teach only one or they can teach multiple courses during a semester. However, future courses are not always assured. Adjuncts usually do not receive benefits such as health, life, or disability insurance nor do they receive employer contributions for retirement." (Ruben, n.d., para. 1)

My definition of an adjunct instructor is "a person who has a passion for teaching, wants to share that passion with others, and is on a contract with one or more universities for one or more courses." Simply, you are a contractor who is given a contract to teach based on course availability and most importantly student enrollments.

Most school's (colleges, institutes, and universities) fiscal year runs from July 1 through June 30. It is my experience that there is more success in obtaining teaching positions in the Fall (Sept–Dec) and Spring (March–May), than during the Summer (June–August). A few summers I have not taught at all—it comes with the territory.

Teaching Terminology

What Romantic terminology called genius or talent or inspiration is nothing other than finding the right road empirically, following one's nose, taking shortcuts.
—Italo Calvino

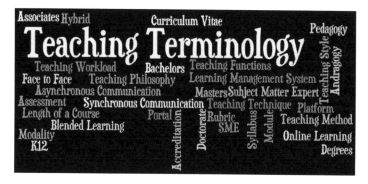

NOTE: The below definitions come from my experience, and I guess you cannot call these definitions, but just plain, simple understanding.

Accreditation—The organizations that ensure schools are following local, state, and federal guidelines.

Andragogy — Adult learning.

Assessment — An assessment is any activity that measures a student's learning.

Asynchronous Communication — This form of communication is like talking on walkie-talkies; I talk, then you talk, but never at the same time.

Curriculum Vitae — Similar to a resume; with the exception that it is more detailed, and is normally used by persons seeking an academic position.

Degree (Associate, Bachelor, Master, Doctorate) — These are the four types of degrees a student can obtain. Additionally, some schools offer certification programs.

Face-to-Face (campus) — Teaching in a classroom where the instructor is standing physically in front of the students.

Hybrid/Blended — A delivery mode of teaching that involves both online teaching and face-to-face teaching.

K12 — This term refers to kindergarten (K) and first through twelfth grade (1-12).

Learning Management Systems — The software system that a school uses to deliver its online/blended learning.

Length of a Course — The measure of time in weeks, a term, semester, or quarter.

Modality — The manner in which a course is taught (e.g., face-to-face, online, blended).

Module — A module is normally equal to a single week when teaching in an online/blended learning format.

Online — Teaching in a virtual classroom that is accessed via the Internet.

Pedagogy — Children's learning.

Portal — A proprietary teaching software for online/hybrid learning.

Platform — Online/hybrid delivery systems are sometimes referred to as a platform.

Rubric — A grading system for course assignments.

SME (Subject Matter Expert) — A person who is considered the expert of a particular subject, function, process, etc.

Syllabus — The road map to what is required in the course, (e.g., teacher's information, required book, weekly assignments, school policies, and more).

Synchronous Communication — Speaking with each other at the same time online.

Teaching Functions — The roles and responsibilities of an adjunct instructor.

Teaching Method — There are three primary teaching methods: face-to-face, blended, and/or online.

Teaching Philosophy—Your reasons for teaching.

Teaching Style—How do you teach? Do you just lecture? Do you stand or sit in front of the class? Do you use technology?

Teaching Technique—This describes what type of teacher you are, (e.g., collaborative, instructivist, behaviorist, etc.).

Teaching Workload—The amount of classes the adjunct instructor teaches at one time.

Teaching Adult Learners

Learn from yesterday,
live for today, hope for tomorrow.
The important thing is to not stop questioning.
Curiosity has its own reason for existing.
—Albert Einstein

Image Credit: 123RF

An adult learner is normally referred to as someone who is of an adult age (18+); however, I have taught students as young as 17 in my college classes. Adult education is for someone who is working on a degree beyond high school (e.g., Associates, Bachelor's, Master's, and/or Doctorate). Therefore, the education level and life experience breadth of a class of adult learners is broad. A class may consist of someone in his/her teens and go up to someone in his/her 70s+, (the oldest student I have had the privilege of learning with is currently 77, and what an inspiration he is).

Teaching adults is completely different than teaching K12 students, but comes with the same challenges of motivating someone to learn and keeping a student engaged. Adult education brings moments of incredible satisfaction, with moments of great frustration—K12 students "have" to be educated; however, adult education or post-secondary education is a *choice*. And with choices, come all of the internal and external factors that determine whether a learner is successful.

I have compiled a list of twelve things you "need to know" as an adjunct instructor, when teaching adult learners. I have gone into detail on the first six.

My List Is:
1. Values
2. Generations
3. Motivation
4. Life Experiences
5. Work Experiences
6. Technical Proficiency
7. Learning Styles
8. Self-directed Learning
9. Collaborative Learning
10. Communication Styles
11. Introvert versus Extrovert
12. Priorities

Values

Image credit: 123RF

I list values as important to teaching an adult learner because it is values which identify us as individuals. Dr. Massey (1990-2005), who is one of my favorite sociologists, discusses, in detail, in his work on generations: it is our values that develop us. He teaches that there are nine external factors that affect our values: (1) family, (2) friends, (3) religion, (4) technology, (5) school, (6) media-advertising, (7) music, (8) income, and (9) geography.

It is important to know the values of your adult learners—the more you know about them as an individual, the easier it is to help them to learn. Notice I did not say "teach" them.

Generations

Image credit: 123RF

I love all things about generational studies, and it is my opinion that it is important, if not critical, to know the generational makeup of the adult learners in my classes. It is the first time in American history that as a nation we have six living generations, and four of those generations are in the workplace; therefore, causing a fun time in the fields of leadership, organizational behavior, organizational development, and human resource management and development.

There are several different studies on the generations in America and each differs slightly in the date range of each generation. Below is a brief list of the six living generations in America:

- *The GI Generation* (1901 - 1924)

- *Veterans (Vets)* also known as the Silent or Traditionalist Generation (1925 - 1943)
- *The Baby Boomers* (1944 - 1960)
- *Generation-X* also known as Gen-X or Busters (1961 - 1979)
- *Generation-Y* also known as Gen-Y, Millennials, Echo Boomers, and many others (1980 - 1999)
- *Generation-Z* also known as the Digital Generation, Homeland Generation, Vacant Generation (2000 - Present)

To learn more about Generations in the Workplace, download my **FREE** PowerPoint from **http://www.slideshare.net/mpostphd**. It is filled with additional resources on the subject.

Motivation

Image Credit: 123RF

I was once told by one of my mentors that one person could not motivate another person, for the definition of motivation involves the "act of behavior." And the word "act" is an action that must be taken on the part of an individual. As a teacher, I can only influence a learner's motivation, but I *cannot* motivate them.

One of my favorite books about motivation is Daniel Pink's book, *Drive*. Check out this **YouTube** video from Daniel's book:
http://www.youtube.com/watch?v=u6XAPnuFjJc

Life Experiences

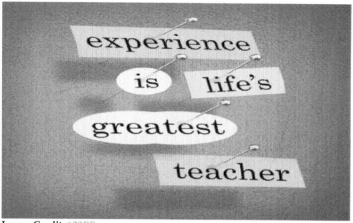

Image Credit: 123RF

Knowing the life experiences of the adult learners in my classes is just as critical as understanding the generations. The one thing I cannot bring into the classroom is the learner's life experiences; and it is these life experiences that add great richness to the learning of the class as a whole.

Work Experiences

Image Credit: 123RF

The work experiences of the adult learner are also crucial in creating a rich learning environment. To know what each learner has done in his/her life is important for building a foundation of existing knowledge in the classroom.

Technical Proficiency

Image Credit: 123RF

Technical proficiency, to me, is necessary for any adult learner. However, not all adult learners have the same level of technical experiences. Technical proficiency is not just limited to the older adult learner. I have experienced adult learners from the ages of 18 to 75, from associates to doctoral degree, having issues with technology.

Because of the availability of technology today, it is assumed everyone knows technology; especially how to use the Internet, write research papers, use the Microsoft Office Suite, and use email. This is not the case with all adult learners.

One of the first lessons I teach in all my classes is about the technology we will be using in the class: how to setup Microsoft Word to write a paper, how to use the Internet to research, and how to use the online classroom. I have learned from experience; I never assume that the adult learners in my classes all understand technology and how to use it.

There are several great websites I recommend to my adult learners if he/she is having issues with technology. One of my favorites is **GCFLearnFree** [http://www.gcflearnfree.org/]. This site provides FREE video tutorials on every Microsoft Office application from 2003 to 2010. Additionally, it has video lectures about the Internet, social media, math, reading, and more. Over 750 videos in all.

Learning Style

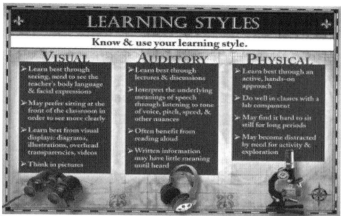

Image Credit: Wiki - EducationalJargonSchs

What is a learning style? Well, the main three that are taught are: (1) auditory (hear), (2) visual (see), and (3) kinesthetic or tactile (physical). However, there are others too. There is active versus reflective learning, sensing versus intuitive learning, and sequential versus global learning. An adult learner may use a combination of all of these in learning his/her course material; an instructor needs to know which styles each adult learner uses, in order to more adequately teach.

One of my favorite and most detailed Learning Styles test, I use is the North Carolina State University Index of Learning Styles Questionnaire, **http://www.engr.ncsu.edu/learningstyles/ilsweb .html**, and it is completely FREE.

In today's classroom, whether it is face-to-face, blended, or fully online, it is important to know the learning style of the adult learner. I state this because as an educator it is my responsibility to ensure I am reaching all the learners through each of their learning styles. This might mean the use of PowerPoint and video for visual learners, classroom discussions for auditory learners, and hands-on activities for the tactile learner.

Adult learners learn differently, and it is the responsibility of the teacher to reach all different types of learners through the variety of learning styles.

Types of Schools

The principle goal of education in the schools should be creating men and women who are capable of doing new things, not simply repeating what other generations have done.
—Jean Piaget

Image Credit - 123RF

Not all schools are created equally in higher education. There are public and private schools; some only teach undergraduate degrees, others only teach graduate degrees, and finally others teach from associate all the way to doctorate. Each school comes with different types of students, administrators, systems, technology, and so much more. It is important to understand each type and identify the one(s) you want to apply to for an adjunct instructor position.

To learn more about the definitions or classifications of each type of school, I encourage you to visit the **Carnegie Foundation for the Advancement of Teaching** (http://www.carnegiefoundation.org) – for as one of my colleagues told me, *"It is the bible for higher ed."*

The Carnegie Foundation does list six all-inclusive classifications:

- **Undergraduate Instructional Program Classification**

- **Graduate Instructional Program Classification**

- **Enrollment Profile Classification**

- **Undergraduate Profile Classification**

- **Size & Setting Classification**

- **Basic Classification**

For a really clear and informative flowchart of these six classifications, with a total number of schools represented in each classification, go to:

http://classifications.carnegiefoundation.org/downloads/2010classifications_logic.pdf

Types of Teaching Methods

More important than the curriculum
is the question of the methods of teaching
and the spirit in which the teaching is given.
—Bertrand Russell

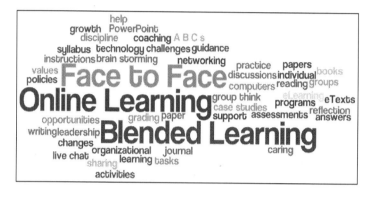

Face-to-Face teaching is traditional classroom teaching. The teacher meets with his/her students in a classroom and the work is submitted via the classroom.

Blended teaching is a combination of traditional face-to-face classroom interaction and online interaction. The adjunct instructor must be able to teach in both methods.

Online teaching takes place via an online platform referred to as a learning management system. The adjunct instructor never interacts with the class face-to-face; however, because of technology advancements, an adjunct instructor can now have face-to-face interactions with their students, but still all online—all work and interaction is accomplished online.

In my opinion, blended and online teaching are more difficult, and I state this mainly because of the increased technologies that an adjunct instructor must learn and use.

Types of Degrees and Certifications

Remember that our nation's first great leaders were also our first great scholars.
—John F. Kennedy

Image Credit - 123RF

There are many types of degrees (see the Carnegie Foundation description for **Undergraduate** [**http://classifications.carnegiefoundation.org/descriptions/ugrad_program.php**] and **Graduate** [**http://classifications.carnegiefoundation.org/descriptions/grad_program.php**] degrees) that consist of associate's, bachelor's, master's, and doctorate degree. In addition to degrees are specialized certifications that schools offer for learners wanting to improve his/her skills, but do not want a full college degree.

Associate's—This degree is considered an undergraduate degree and normally takes about 2-years to complete. An associate's degree can be completed at most community colleges and career colleges. What is a career college? A career college is a vocational or trade school. An associate's degree can be defined as an AA (Associate of Arts), AS (Associate of Science), AAS (Associate of Applied Science), and AGS (Associate of General Studies).

Bachelor's—This degree is normally a 4-year degree and it too is an undergraduate degree. There are four types of bachelor's degree, BA (Bachelor of Arts), BS (Bachelor of Science), BFA (Bachelor of Fine Arts), and BBA (Bachelor of Business Administration).

Master's—This degree normally takes 2-years to complete and the student must have completed a bachelor's before pursuing a master's degree. The most popular types of master's degree are, MBA (Master of Business Administration), MS (Master of Science), MA (Master of Arts), MED (Master of Education), and MAT (Master of Arts in Teaching). However, this is not all the different types of master's degrees.

Doctoral—This degree normally takes 3-5 years to complete, but the length depends on the program and the student's dissertation topic. There are many types of doctoral degrees, the most common are the PhD (Doctor of Philosophy), EdD (Doctor of Education), DBA (Doctor of Business Administration), PsyD (Doctor of Psychology), and DMin (Doctor of Ministry).

Certificate—Many schools offer certificate programs in specific areas (e.g., leadership, social media, vocation specific areas), and these certificate programs require only a certain amount of courses and hours. Certificate programs are a great way for professional development.

What is Accreditation?

The main part of intellectual education is not the acquisition of facts but learning how to make facts live.
—Oliver Wendell Holmes

Image Credit - 123RF

When a school receives accreditation, it is an acknowledgement from an accrediting body for meeting academic excellence. There are many types of accrediting agencies—a school can achieve local, national, regional, and/or program specific accreditations. Schools go through great pains to achieve and maintain accreditation, and I always recommend teaching for a school that has the highest accreditation to teach for. It is important to do your research when researching schools that you want to teach for; because you do not want to teach for what is known as a "diploma mill" where degrees are *given*, not earned. Below is a list of accrediting agencies, I encourage you to review some of the sites to gain a greater understanding of accrediting. (Before you base your application to teach strictly upon the accreditation of a school, remember that some schools seek no accreditation at all.

Federal Agencies
- The U.S. Department of Education, **http://www.ed.gov/**

Regional Accreditors
- Middle States Association of Colleges and Schools (MSCHE), **http://msche.org/**
- New England Association of Schools and Colleges (NEASC-CIHE) Commission on Institutions of Higher Education, **http://cihe.neasc.org/**
- (NEASC-CTCI) Commission on Technical and Career Institutions, **http://cihe.neasc.org/**
- Northwest Commission on Colleges and Universities (NWCCU), **http://www.nwccu.org/**
- Higher Learning Commission (North Central Association of Colleges and Schools) (NCA-HLC), **http://www.ncahlc.org/**

- Southern Association of Colleges and Schools (SACS) Commission on Colleges, **http://sacs.org/**
- Western Association of Schools and Colleges (WASC-ACCJC) Accrediting Commission for Community and Junior Colleges, **http://www.accjc.org/**
- (WASC-ACSCU) Accrediting Commission for Senior Colleges and Universities, **http://www.wascsenior.org/**

National Accreditors
- Accrediting Bureau of Health Education Schools (ABHES), **http://www.abhes.org/**
- Accrediting Commission of Career Schools and Colleges (ACCSC), **http://www.accsc.org/**

Accreditation Requirements to Be an Adjunct Instructor

The best teacher is the one who suggests rather than dogmatizes, and inspires his listener with the wish to teach himself.
—Edward Bulwer-Lytton

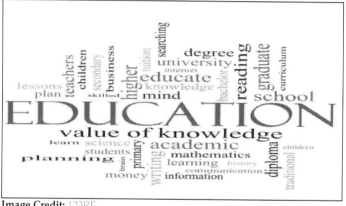

Image Credit: 123RF

Each Institution will have specific requirements based on its Accreditation and State regulations. To teach at a bachelor's level, a bachelor's degree may be the only requirement, and/or a master's degree may be required to teach a bachelor's program.

Each institution is really different in the requirements. One university I teach for requires a combination of a master's degree and industry experience in order to teach at its master's level. Moreover, another university I teach for only allows you to teach for the university if you have a doctoral degree.

In my experience, the higher the degree I have, the more opportunities I have to teach at all levels and at a variety of institutions.

Length of an Adjunct Teaching Position

They inspire you, they entertain you, and you end up learning a ton even when you don't know it.
—Nicholas Sparks

Image Credit - 123RF

Each school has different term, semester, and/or quarter length. For example, a school may have 5 weeks, 6, 7, 8, 9, 10, 11, 12, 15, and 16 week length term/semester/quarter. It is possible to teach every term/semester/quarter, or in some cases, an adjunct instructor may only teach once a year for a school.

For example, I currently am in the adjunct pool for various schools, but may only be teaching once a year for some, and every term for others. If you want to be adjunct full-time, it is necessary to be in multiple adjunct pools, not just one. The cliché is true when teaching as a full-time adjunct: "*You cannot put all your eggs into one basket.*" I have been "burned" when I did.

STEP 2

LANDING

Your Adjunct
Instructor Position

Identifying Your Motives for Becoming an Adjunct Instructor

The mediocre teacher tells.
The good teacher explains.
The superior teacher demonstrates.
The great teacher inspires.
—William Arthur Ward

Image Credit: 123RF

What I am about to say, will sound harsh, and I will apologize now. IF the only reason you want to be an Adjunct Instructor is so that you can make extra money, *please do not become one.* I say this, for it truly affects your ability to teach, if it is only driven from a motivation of money. Not all people are called to teach or even have the abilities to teach. I will also say this: *"If you are a good Adjunct Instructor and have a passion for it, the money will come."* I have seen this in my own career as an Adjunct Instructor.

If you asked yourself why you want to become an Adjunct Instructor and your answer was to share that which you have learned, then I believe your heart is that of a teacher and you do have something to share that others need to learn—the money will follow.

Understanding
What's in Store for You

*What the teacher is, is more important
than what he teaches.*
—Karl A. Menninger

Image Credit: 123RF

Before we jump right in on how to begin building
your Adjunct Platform, I feel you need to know
what's in store for you. Days will be filled with
late night grading, in order to meet deadlines,
giving up weekends (not all the time, but some of
the time), utilization of technology—many bad
student evaluations, frustration when students do
not turn in their homework on time, and not always the greatest pay.

However, that is not all; you will see your students walk across the stage in their cap and gown

upon their successful graduation, receiving great student reviews, constant learning, constant growing, and an incredible satisfaction of making a difference in someone's life. So, if you are ready to build your Adjunct Instructor Platform, then take a life-long rewarding journey with me. Allow me to be your guiding architect as you Build Your Adjunct Platform.

Creating a Teaching Resume

*Better than a thousand days of diligent study
is one day with a great teacher.*
—Japanese Proverb

Image Credit - 123RF

Let me first say, *"I am not a resume expert"* and I cannot *guarantee* the success of any of the suggestions that I am recommending you use on your resume. I know what has worked for *me*, or honestly, what I like on my resume. I do recommend a *second resume* for teaching for as you begin adding new teaching positions, it will easily highlight your abilities.

In academia, a teacher's experience is highlighted with a Curriculum Vitae (CV). However, I did not come from academia, so I still refer to mine as a teaching resume—it just works for me. I like my resume, and have had good success with it. However, I am certain there have been some that did not like my resume because I have been turned down for more teaching jobs then I have held.

What are schools looking for in an adjunct teacher?

The easiest way to answer this question is to do your research. Here is an example:

1. Go to the following website:
http://www.higheredjobs.com/
2. Enter the keywords for "*adjunct instructor*"
3. Review the results, select one that is in your field of expertise (Example: I would search on business, leadership, HR, technology)
4. Read the requirements of the job and ask yourself the simple question: "*Can I do this requirement?*" If your answer is "yes," then that information should be featured on your teaching resume.

The components of a teaching resume from my experience are:

- **Personal Information:** *Caution:* I do not give out my phone or address if this is a public resume, I only provide that information if I am filling out an online application or if I received a request for my resume by a specific individual.

- **Social Media Accounts: LinkedIn, Facebook, Twitter,** Blog, Website, or any other social media account that may add a positive experience to who you are.
- **Objective:** I am personally not a fan of an "objective," but again, I am not a resume expert and I know many books discuss the importance of an objective.
- **Qualifications:** In this section is where I highlight those "specific" job abilities that a school is looking for. If I have designed and delivered training, then I am going to state it in this section.
- **Education:** List your degrees with highest to lowest, e.g., Doctorate, Master's, Bachelor's, Associate's.
- **Certifications:** List any industry specific certifications, e.g., PMP, LCP, MCSE, etc.
- **Technical Skills:** I provide this area because my background is technical, and I list the hardware, software, and learning management systems that I know well.
- **Professional Memberships:** List all the professional organizations that you are a current member of, e.g., American Society of Training and Development, etc.
- **Publications:** This is one of the main differences between a curriculum vitae and a resume. In academia, a publication section is included for the listing of research work, articles published, and/or books pub-

lished. If you do not have any publications, do not include this section on your resume.

- **Teaching Experience:** List your teaching experience and break it out via face-to-face, online, and blended.

  - o **NOTE:** If you do not have teaching experience, then list within your professional experience where you have developed and delivered training, (e.g., you were a speaker for an event, performed research, etc.)

- **Professional Experience:** List your professional experiences and highlight applicable skills and job functions that would aid you in being an adjunct instructor.

TIPS:

- Use a professional template—this can be accomplished by using Microsoft Word's Resume templates. The program actually has one for teaching. Additionally, do some Internet searches for examples of teaching resumes, like the ones listed below.

  - o Craft an Effective Teacher Resume— **http://www.scribd.com/doc/9799551 8/Road-to-Teaching-Craft-an-Effective-Teacher-Resume**

- o This site actually has a template you can download, and I think it is a great template—**http://career-advice.careerone.com.au/resume-cover-letter/sample-resume/cv-template-school-teacher/article.aspx**
- **Save** the resume both as a Microsoft Word document (HINT: I always recommend saving as MS Word 2003 ".doc" to ensure it is compatible with all versions of Microsoft Word).
- Finally, save the resume as a **PDF file**. This is the industry standard—save all documents that you will be sending and updating as a PDF.
  - o To save a Microsoft Word document as a PDF, complete the following steps:
    1) Select SAVE AS from the file menu 2) select PDF, and 3) select Publish.
  - o Now you have both a MS Word document and a PDF of your resume.

Being Creative with Your Resume

We are more than role models for our students;
we are leaders and teachers of both an academic
curriculum and a social curriculum.
—Patricia Sequeira Belvel

Image Credit: 123RF

It is not enough in today's fast-paced, social media driven world to have a "normal" resume—you need to stand out. Some additional ways to do this is to be playful with your resume. Please take heed though, this may not be for the timid of heart, or for persons who do not like change and do not like thinking out of the box. *So how can you stand out?*

- **Adding a Wordle** (word cloud) to your resume. The below is a "Wordle" that I created for myself and I have added to the top of my resume and it is the first item you see on my resume.

- **Creating a visual resume,** go to VisualCV—**http://www.visualcv.com/www/ind exc.html** or **VisualizeMe**: **http://vizualize.me/**

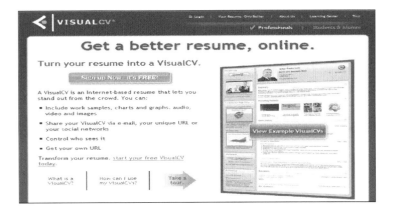

- **Create a video** and upload to **YouTube** or **Vimeo** to go along with your submitted resume; or use a tool like **ResumeTube**: **http://www.resumetube.com/**.

- **Create a presentation resume** or Presume, go to **SlideRocket** to see what a Presume is: **http://www.sliderocket.com/blog/2011/11/presentation-resume/**

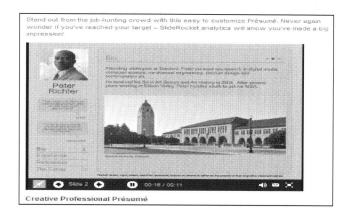

Writing Your Teaching Cover Letter

Teachers open the door,
but you must enter by yourself.
—Chinese Proverb

Image Credit: 123RF

I will state again, "I am not an *expert* in writing cover letters," but I have written so many that I have a good feel for what works and what doesn't. Below are *my* suggestions on what a teaching cover letter could contain.

- **Step 1:** First, a cover letter is a first impression of who you are. If the hiring manager likes your cover letter, then he/she will want to review your resume, but the opposite is also true.

- **Step 2:** Quick tips for cover letter success: (1) personalized letterhead, (2) professionally written, no grammar or spelling errors, (3) concise (1-page ONLY), (4) a pitch of who you are and what you can do, and (5) respectful.
- **Step 3:** Write the cover letter on professional letterhead, this can easily be created using Microsoft Word's letterhead templates.
- **Step 4:** Begin with your information: Name, Address, Phone Number, Email Address.
- **Step 5:** It is always better to have a specific person to address the cover letter to, but if you do not have the hiring person's name, I always use "Dear Sir or Madam." I feel using "To Whom It May Concern" is just lazy and does not show a desire to really get the job, but that is my opinion (not an expert's).
- **Step 6:** A powerful opening that states the position you are seeking and why. SELL IT!
- **Step 7:** Three, to maybe five, brief bullet points of who you are and what you can do, and do not repeat this on your resume, use "new material" here. Statistics speak volumes. Do not just state you are a good communicator, instead demonstrate that with statistical data, e.g., "Research, writ-

ten and presented to an audience of 60+ on the topic of Social Media in Education." This is showing, not just telling.

- **Step 8:** Provide a closing that is "aggressive" but not arrogant. Let the hiring manager know you will be contacting them in so many days to answer any questions — do not state, "Hope to hear from you soon." SELL IT!

- **Step 9:** End with a thank you to the hiring manager for taking the time to read and review your resume.

- **Step 10:** Sign with a "Sincerely," and make sure you sign the cover letter. This is where I encourage fellow colleagues who create a digital signature, so that he/she can sign electronic documents.

- **Step 11:** Use Microsoft Word's advanced grammar and spell checking features to ensure that the cover letter is grammatically correct and contains no spelling errors.
  - o To learn how to set Microsoft Word's Advanced Editing features, download my FREE slideshare.net presentation

     http://www.slideshare.net/mpostph d/ms-word-advanced-editing-for-apa-v1 (Even though the title states for APA 6th edition, following the steps in this presentation will allow you to set Advanced Editing features in MS Word 2003, 2007, and 2010. The presentation is FREE!)

- **Step 12:** Save the cover letter both as a Microsoft Word document (HINT: I always recommend saving as MS Word 2003 ".doc" to ensure it is compatible with later versions of Microsoft Word—2007, 2010).
- **Step 13:** Finally, save the cover letter as a PDF file. This is the industry standard—save all documents that you will be sending and updating as a PDF.
  - To save a Microsoft Word document as a PDF, complete the following steps:
  - (1) Select SAVE AS from the file menu,
    (2) Select PDF, and
    (3) Select Publish.

    Now you have both a MS Word document and a PDF of your cover letter.

Asking for Recommendation Letters

You cannot teach a man anything,
you can only help him find it within himself.
—Galileo

Image Credit: 123RF

When you are applying for an adjunct instructor position on a school's website, I have always encountered where the site asks for at least three letters of recommendation. It is important to ask people you know and trust that will provide you with a strong recommendation letter. When asking someone for a recommendation letter, let the person know that you are seeking an adjunct instructor position. If you receive the letter as a "physical" hardcopy, I would recommend scanning it so that you can create an electronic copy to be stored on your computer's hard disk.

Check out this blog post about asking for a "reference/recommendation" letter:
http://www.scholarlyhires.com/Applicant/Articles/Letters-of-Reference-Part-1-What-Do-Readers-W

Asking for Recommendations on LinkedIn

Seek opportunities to show you care.
The smallest gestures often make the biggest difference.
—John Wooden

Let me recommend again, if you do not have a **LinkedIn** account, I highly recommend that you create one. It is a great way to create your professional profile, your professional platform, and your adjunct platform. In my humble opinion, a **LinkedIn** account is a *"must have"* in your job search toolbox. If you do not believe me, check out this blog post, *"Recruiters Say: Avoid LinkedIn at Your Peril"*:
http://www.forbes.com/sites/work-in-progress/2012/05/11/recruiters-say-avoid-linkedin-at-your-peril/

I encourage you to review the following blog posts about asking for a **LinkedIn** Recommendation. **LinkedIn** recommends that you have at least three recommendations to have a complete profile.

Suggested LinkedIn Reading:

- How to ask for **LinkedIn** recommendations: **http://www.keppiecareers.com/2011/01/16/how-to-ask-for-linkedin-recommendations/**
- Everything You Need to Know About LinkedIn Recommendations: **http://www.forbes.com/sites/susanadams/2012/02/08/everything-you-need-to-know-about-linkedin-recommendations/**
- 6 Things You Need to Know About LinkedIn
- Recommendations: **http://mashable.com/2012/05/16/linkedin-recommendations/**
- How to Write a LinkedIn Recommendation: **http://www.wikihow.com/Write-a-LinkedIn-Recommendation**

TIP: The rule of thumb is if someone has provided you a recommendation, you return the favor. We all need to help one another out in this socially networked world.

Asking for Endorsements
on LinkedIn

It is clearly absurd to limit the term 'education'
to a person's formal schooling.
—Murray N. Rothbard

NOTE: The faces of the endorsements have been blotted out for the individual's protection.

LinkedIn has a new feature—**Endorsements**, and I love how they referred to it on their blog, "give kudos with just one click." The new Endorsement feature is as simple as a single click. However, the **Skills & Expertise** Section on your profile has to be completed with what you consider to be your top skills.

Here is what you do:

Steps: Adding Skills & Expertise to Your Profile

1. Log into your **LinkedIn** profile
2. Select the **Profile** from the menu list
3. Select **Edit Profile**
4. Find **Skills & Expertise** on your profile (scroll down the page, it is toward the bottom of your profile)
5. Select the **Edit** button next to **Skills & Expertise**
6. To add a skill, click in the box and begin typing your first skill. As you begin typing, skills will appear and you can select from a list or write in your own. Click the **Add** button to add the new skill.
7. After you have added the skill into your list, click on the skill and you will be prompted to select the level of proficiency and years of experience. After selecting these two criteria, close the window by clicking in the upper right corner of the small pop-up window.
8. Continue adding your best skills one at a time. Per **LinkedIn,** you can only add 50 skills.
9. When you have added all the skills you want, make sure to click the **SAVE** button on the bottom left corner. (see screen shot below)

NOTE: Add your Skills & Expertise by top priority, so really ly think about this before just adding skills (I did not know that fact until after I added my skills).

Steps: Requesting Endorsements from Your Contacts

1. Email your Level-1 network connections and ask if they would endorse you for specific skills or all your skills.

2. It is easy for your network connections to endorse your Skills & Expertise. When someone from your Level-1 network connections views your profile, he/she will be prompted at the top of the page with the opportunity to endorse your skills or he/she can even add a skill to your profile.

3. A second way to endorse one of your network connections is to "View Profile," go to Skills & Expertise section, Select the Skill you would like to endorse and click on the little blue plus sign on the right of the skill, then you will have endorsed your network

connection and he/she will be notified with an email.

Suggested Reading: Here is a list of great blog postings that teaches more about the new Endorsement feature of LinkedIn:

- LinkedIn—Introducing One Click Endorse-dorse-ments—**http://www.slideshare.net/linkedin/introducing-linkedin-endorsements**
- Social Media Examiner—6 Tips for Using LinkedIn the New Endorsements—**http://www.socialmediaexaminer.com/linkedin-endorsements/**
- LinkedIn's Blog—Introducing Endorsements: Give Kudos With Just One Click—**http://blog.linkedin.com/2012/09/24/introducing-endorsements-give-kudos-with-just-one-click/**
- Entrepreneur—3 Tips for Using LinkedIn's New 'Endorsements'—**http://www.entrepreneur.com/blog/224512**
- Digital Trends—Introducing Endorsements: A new way to be recognized for skills and expertise—**http://www.digitaltrends.com/social-media/linkedin-rolls-out-skill-endorsements-and-its-as-easy-as-one-click/**

Asking for References

*I never teach my pupils, I only attempt to provide
the conditions in which they can learn.*
—Albert Einstein

Image Credit: 123RF

There are at least two types of references: professional and personal; and it is important, in my opinion (not necessarily the expert's), to have both. Additionally, professional references need to consist of persons who were, or are, your supervisor, your direct reports, and peer colleagues. This provides a well-rounded list of professional references.

I keep a list of my professional and personal references. I update it no less than once a year—I try to do it more often. I always make sure that I have asked each person if I can use him or her as either a professional reference or personal reference. This is important because if you list someone as a professional reference, and they are a personal reference, it could be embarrassing when the hiring manager contacts them and asks questions they cannot answer.

It would also be beneficial to send a copy of your CV and resume to everyone, both personal and professional, who has agreed to be a reference for you. Having your accomplishments in front of them refreshes their memory about your abilities and is a subtle reminder to keep you in mind for any suitable job opportunities they might come across.

Here are my steps for creating a Reference List:

- **Step 1:** Create a Microsoft Word document with a table that has two columns: (1) professional references and (2) personal references.
- **Step 2:** List each reference in the appropriate table with their name and degree title or their certification/licensure, current company, phone number, and email address.
- **Step 3:** Do the same for your personal references.

- **Step 4:** How many references? In my experience, most of the schools I have applied for require at least three, but I always have my list of references with five listed under each category.

Professional References	Personal References
John Doe, Ph.D. ABC University Email: jdoe@abc.edu Phone: 555-555-5555	Jane Smith Consultant Email: jane@myco.com Phone: 555-555-1234
Bob Smith, MBA Adjunct Faculty Email: bsmith@univ.edu Phone: 555-555-4321	Tom Doe, CPA Adjunct Faculty Email: tdoe@school.edu Phone: 555-555-1212

Here are some tips when asking for references:

- Ask for professional and personal references from people you respect and trust. Why ask someone who doesn't like you? The goal is to get the job.
- Ask your reference if you can use them and let them know what position you are seeking. It doesn't hurt to let the references know what you are applying for; in fact, it helps them to know so he/she knows how to answer the hiring manager's questions.

- Ask your reference for the information that he/she is more comfortable with providing, and make sure you write it down accurately.
- Always thank your references for being a reference.
- Don't be afraid to change your references, it is okay and you should, especially if you change companies.
- Update your references at least once a year.
- Check out this blog post: **Tips for Asking for Job References— http://pinnacle.jobs/tips-for-asking-for-job-references/**

Writing Your Teaching Philosophy

*I'm not a teacher: only a fellow traveler of whom you
asked the way. I pointed ahead—
ahead of myself as well as you.*
—George Bernard Shaw

Image Credit: 123RF

You may be asking yourself, *"What is a teaching
philosophy?"* The easiest answer I can give is *"Why
do you teach?"* Do you teach because you have a
passion for it? Do you teach because you love
learning and want to share that learning? What-
ever your motives are, this becomes your teaching
philosophy. Many schools will ask for this as one
of the supporting documents that are required
when applying for a position—it is normally 1-1.5
pages or about 500 words. Below is my teaching
philosophy:

My philosophy revolves around the fact that I am a servant teacher who is learner centered. I believe all students have incredible potential, and it is my job as a teacher to aid them in releasing their potential through the subject matter I am teaching. I say I am a servant teacher because I am a servant leader and I believe the more I serve and lift those around me, the more I am lifted up to becoming a better teacher and leader. I am learner centered because education is about the learner, not the educator. It is my responsibility to create and deliver fresh information with every class period to ensure the learners are getting the best I can deliver. My faith also teaches me, those who take on the responsibility of teaching will be judged twice as hard, so I take teaching seriously and know it is not only the students to whom I am answering.

To be a good teacher, I believe one must love the students, just as to be a good leader, one must love people. I refer to both teacher and leader in my philosophy for I believe I cannot be one without the other. As a teacher, I am required to lead those whom I teach and aid them in performing at their best so they will leave the classroom with new knowledge that can be applied to new experiences. When I stand in front of a class of learners, I have to realize it is not about how much I know, but instead about what I do not know, but am willing to learn, to ensure the students has room to grow.

I am honest and upfront with the students I have the privilege of teaching. I teach them each of us has a part in this relationship, and we can be successful only if both of us do our part. Teaching is not just about the material, but about the relationships built with the students, the life lessons incorporated within the material and the model being created to show students the world is not to change for them, but they are to change for the world. I teach them in the words of Gandhi, "Be the change you want to see in the world."

I believe students will respond when they realize how much a teacher cares, not just how much a teacher knows. Borrowing the words of President Theodore Roosevelt, "No one cares how much you know, until they know how much you care." I do care about teaching, but more importantly, I care about students. To me, teaching is a double-edge sword of gratification and frustration. When I do not reach a student, I become frustrated and tell myself I cannot reach them all. However, when I do reach a student, it is a great achievement for both of us.

Identifying the Subject(s)
You Can Teach

Teachers have three loves: love of learning,
love of learners, and the love of bringing
the first two loves together.
—Scott Hayden

Image Credit: 123RF

What is it you want to teach? On the other hand, I should ask the question, "What is it you are *qualified* to teach?" Accrediting bodies of schools have specific requirements regarding how many hours an adjunct instructor must prove in his/her degrees, in order to teach a specific subject.

I would love to teach a course in history, just because I love it, but unfortunately, I am not qualified to teach history because I do not have the accrediting requirements. It is important to verify that you can teach specific subjects based on the specific hours in your degree(s). For example, if you want to teach marketing, but your bachelor's is in psychology and your master's is in accounting, it does not mean you have the accrediting qualifications to teach marketing.

When applying for adjunct teaching positions, make sure that you have the right amount of accrediting hours. The most common accrediting rule is a teacher must have at least 18-hours in the subject matter he/she wants to teach. However, many times this is waived if the instructor has the industry experience, i.e., CPA, Attorney, etc.

Do not make the mistake I made when I first began teaching, take on everything offered. This was the worst thing I could to the students and myself. I accepted courses that I could learn and then teach what I learn, but this is not a good practice. Teach what you know! Learners can tell when a teacher knows or does not know the material.

Identify Your Network
of Potential Contacts

A candle loses nothing by lighting another candle.
—Erin Majors

Image Credit: 123RF

The cliché is true when it comes to landing your first adjunct teaching position: *"It's who you know."* I will share my experience with you and say it was very difficult landing my first adjunct instructor position, for two reasons: (1) I did not have a teaching background, and (2) I did not know any current adjuncts or educators that could help me get a "foot in the door." Therefore, I was turned down many times; but I will say, once you get that first position and are successful in it, you will obtain others more easily.

LinkedIn is one of the best places to start identifying your network of potential contacts. If you do not have a **LinkedIn** account, as I have stated before, it is time you created one. (I have made several book recommendations in the Resource section including book(s) for getting started with **LinkedIn**.)

If you do not have a **LinkedIn** account, then I recommend making a list of your potential contacts. Take a piece of paper, or open a Word document or even an Excel spreadsheet and begin "brainstorming" on who you know. Do you know anyone who is a current adjunct, and where? Are any of the teachers who you took courses from still working for the school? Do you know anyone, who "knows" someone who is a current adjunct and would be willing to make an introduction for you? Have you utilized your school's Career Services?

Here is a list of some of my favorite books on the topics of referrals and networking:

- *Career Distinction: Stand Out by Building Your Brand*, William Arruda and Kirsten Dixson
- *Linchpin: Are You Indispensable?*, Seth Godin

- *Make Your Contacts Count: Networking Know-how for Business and Career Success (2nd Edition)*, Anne Baber and Lynne Waymon
- *Me 2.0, Revised and Updated Edition: 4 Steps to Building Your Future*, Dan Schawbel
- *Platform: Get Noticed in a Noisy World*, Michael Hyatt
- *Smart Networking, Attract a Following in Person and Online*, Liz Lynch
- *The 29% Solution: 52 Weekly Networking Success Strategies*, Ivan Misner and Michelle R. Donovan
- *What Color is Your Parachute? 2013: A Practical Manual for Job-Hunters and Career-Changers*, Richard N. Bolles
- *What Color Is Your Parachute? Guide to Job-Hunting Online, (6th Edition): Blogging, Career Sites, Gateways, Getting Interviews, Job Boards, Job Search ... Resumes, Research Sites, Social Networking*, Mark Emery Bolles and Richard N. Bolles

Creating Your Adjunct Instructor Packet

You can never be overdressed or overeducated.
—Oscar Wilde

One of the many tools I have developed as an Adjunct Instructor is creating my Adjunct Instructor Packet. I use the packet each time I apply for a new adjunct instructor position. Below are the steps and recommended documents I have in my Adjunct Instructor Packet:

- **Step 1:** Create a folder on your computer and label it "Adjunct Packet"
- **Step 2:** Under the "Adjunct Instructor Packet" folder create the following sub-folders (see screen shot below).
    - Certifications & Licensures
    - Professional Development
    - Recommendations and References
    - Resume & Cover Letter
    - Teaching Philosophy

- Transcripts

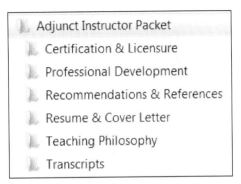

- **Step 3:** Copy your teaching resume and cover letter into the folder labeled "Resume & Cover Letter."
- **Step 4:** Make copies of your transcripts or download official or unofficial transcripts and copy them into the folder labeled "Transcripts." To make electronic copies of your official transcripts you can use a scanner and scan them into your computer.
- **Step 5:** Make electronic copies of every certification or licensure that you have completed and copy them into the folder labeled "Certifications & Licensures."
- **Step 6:** Copy your teaching philosophy into the folder labeled "Teaching Philosophy."
- **Step 7:** Copy your recommendation letters and your list of references into the folder labeled "Recommendations & References."

- **Step 8:** Download my *"Professional Development Tracker.pdf"* Template from the following location: **http://reachyourpotential.info/blog/** and copy it into the folder labeled "Professional Development." Each time you complete a workshop, webinar, course, seminar, and or any type of event that "enhances" your current skills, add it to this template. The reason you want to do this is that many schools will ask you for this information at the end of the year, and it is just easier tracking it as you go (see example).

Professional Development Tracking Sheet

Name of Training	Type of Training	Description	Certificate Received	Date of Completion
Social Media Manager Schools	Professional	Online school on how to become a successful Social Media Manager	Test Not Taken	Currently in school
Social Media Examiner Blogger Summit 2012	Personal/Professional	Two week course consisting of live webinars on the various ways to become a successful blogger in business	Yes	August 2012

TIP: After you are hired by a school, creating additional repeatable assets will make your life easier. Examples of these are copies of your social security card, passport, and driver's license. These are all necessary for completing the I-9 paperwork; and instead of copying them as you need them, make additional copies and keep them in a fireproof safe.

Create a Plan of Attack

Live as if you were to die tomorrow.
Learn as if you were to live forever.
—Mahatma Gandhi

Image Credit: 123RF

To land your first adjunct position, you need a plan of attack. It is easy to say, "I am going to become an adjunct instructor," but the bigger question is, "How are you going to become an adjunct instructor?"

Your plan of attack can be simple or in-depth; it depends on what your goals are. Here is an example plan of attack:

- **Step 1:** Create a teaching resume
- **Step 2:** Create a **LinkedIn** account if you do not have one; if you do, then join sever-

al Adjunct Groups (see a list of Adjunct Groups in the Resource section)

- **Step 3:** Listen to the Adjunct Groups on **LinkedIn** and learn from those already in the industry
- **Step 4:** Identify the subject matter you can and want to teach
- **Step 5:** Identify a list of references
- **Step 6:** Request recommendations
- **Step 7:** Create your Adjunct Instructor Packet
- **Step 8:** Identify the schools you want to teach for or that are hiring currently.
  - Ask friends and coworkers if any of them are currently an adjunct; if yes, is their school hiring. Remember, in today's socially networked world, it's who you know.
  - Setup a job alert on **HigherEd Jobs**, **http://www.higheredjobs.com/default.cfm**
  - Looking for only online adjunct positions? Check out the resource list below, or purchase the book, **Schools That Hire Online Adjunct Faculty: An Updated Database for Online Instructors** by Nicolas Veracruz. This book is one large listing of all the schools that hire online adjuncts and the websites to the schools. It is available on **Amazon**.

- **Step 9:** Create Job Alerts to be notified of the teaching positions you are wanting.
    - o Many, if not all job sites, will allow you to setup an email alert when new jobs are available.

    - o Looking for schools in only a particular state? Check out this site, it is from the National Center for Education Statistics and its College Navigator: **http://nces.ed.gov/collegenavigator/** It is easy to navigate through. All I did was select Colorado and it provided a listing of 136 schools in Colorado. In addition, I can narrow the search by degree type and school type (see screen shot).

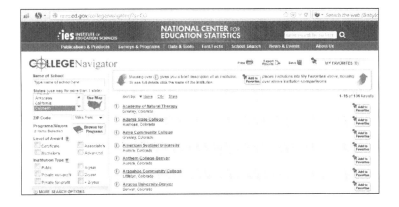

- **Step 10:** Begin applying to various schools that you have a desire to teach for.

TIP: Don't become frustrated and disappointed if you do not land an adjunct instructor position right away, for there are many variables that affect your hiring: (1) teaching experience, (2) skills required, (3) course availability, (4) student enrollments, and (5) competition. I say competition, for in my state, Colorado, there are more persons with a doctorate degree who live in Colorado than any other state in the United States. Therefore, competition is very high, if I am looking to work in a Colorado school.

Other Platform Building Ideas

Education is the most powerful weapon,
which you can use to change the world.
—Nelson Mandela

There are many ways to build, not only your Adjunct Instructor Platform, but also your *personal* platform. Below is a list of other platform building opportunities:

- **Create PowerPoint presentations**—There are many great sites to create or upload and share your PowerPoint presentations. (see below).
    - Slideshare—**Slideshare.net** is a great website for research, but also for publishing PowerPoint presentations that you have created. One of the reasons this is considered platform building is

that you can provide potential school employers the ability to see the work you are doing or have done. Check out my Slideshare account:
http://www.slideshare.net/mpostphd

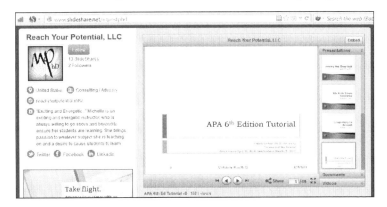

- o Slideboom—
  http://www.slideboom.com/

- AuthorStream—
  http://www.authorstream.com/

- Prezi—
  http://prezi.com/

- Sliderocket —
  http://www.sliderocket.com/

- **Publishing on Paid Content sites** — A paid content site is free to both the contributor and the one searching for content. What these types of sites allow you to do is publish documents, video, audio, and/or photo, and when someone clicks on your content you receive royalties from the paid content host. Some of the top paid content sites are:
  - Yahoo Contributor Network — **https://contributor.yahoo.com/sign up/**
  - Yahoo Voices— **http://voices.yahoo.com/**
  - Triond—**http://www.triond.com/**
  - Helium—**http://www.helium.com/**
  - Wordpreneur— **http://wordpreneur.com/**

- o Scribd—**http://www.scribd.com/**
- o Wikihow—**http://www.wikihow.com/Main-Page**
- o Issuu—**http://issuu.com/**
- o Writer Gazette—**http://www.writergazette.com/view-call-for-submissions**
- o Examiner—**http://www.examiner.com/**
- o eHow (Demand Studios)—**http://www.ehow.com/**
- o Gather—**http://www.gather.com/**
- o Skyword—**http://www.skyword.com/**
- o BrightHub—**http://www.brighthub.com/**
- o About—**http://www.about.com/#!/editors-picks/**
- o AllVoices—**http://www.allvoices.com/**
- o Suite101—**http://suite101.com/**
- o Squidoo—**http://www.squidoo.com/**

- **Hosting your own Blog site**
  - o This is a create blog posting with podcast on how to setup your own blog using **WordPress**.

- How to Launch a Self-Hosted WordPress Blog in 20 Minutes or Less [Screencast]

- **Creating Information Products**—An information product can be created in several different Webinar formats (eBooks, eZines, Newsletters, Reports, Research Data, Whitepapers, and Tutorials (PowerPoint, Video, and Podcast). Due to the Internet, a person's potential for making money on the Internet is only limited by two things: (1) their imagination and (2) their time.

- **Become an ePublisher of "what you know"**—The playing field has been completely leveled when it comes to ePublishing or Self-Publishing and this is one of the easiest ways to build your platform. Check out the Resource section for a list of books on ePublishing.

- **Produce short Videos**—Just like ePublishing, it has never been easier to create and share videos on the web:
  - **Youtube.com**
  - **Vimeo.com**
  - **Google Video**
  - **Yahoo Video**
  - **Hulu.com**
  - **Viddler.com**
  - **MetaCafe.com**

- **Be a Guest Blogger**—Many websites are always looking for "guest bloggers" to write an article or review.
- **Become an Expert**—Use sites like **LinkedIn** to post and answer questions, but take heed—you have to stay active on these types of sites, at least once a week.

STEP 3

KEEPING

Your Adjunct
Instructor Position

Keeping Your Adjunct Position

"We delight in the beauty of the butterfly, but rarely admit the changes it has gone through to achieve that beauty."
—Maya Angelou

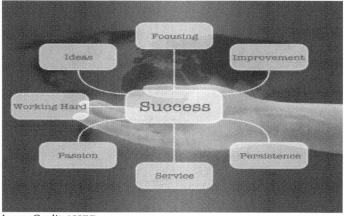

Image Credit: 123RF

It can be easy keeping an adjunct instructor position, but it also can be difficult—it all depends on the priority that you place on your adjunct instructor position. I state this because if it is just an "after thought" job, then it will be difficult maintaining it, for you will never have time to do it right.

Being an adjunct, whether it is for one class or multiple classes, takes time to prepare, deliver, and grade a specific course. In order to be a successful adjunct instructor, you need to ensure that you have the time—desire is not enough. Maintaining an adjunct instructor position requires dedication, accountability, flexibility, willingness to keep on learning and developing yourself, and a lot of work.

However, with that stated, being an adjunct instructor is a very rewarding job and can be easily added to an already busy schedule—it just takes initial planning and preparation. So let's get started to ensure you maintain your adjunct instructor position(s).

Understand Who You Are

Intelligence plus character—
that is the goal of true education.
—Martin Luther King, Jr.

One of the lessons I teach in all my classes, especially my leadership classes is *"know who you are."* What this means is…discovering who you are through various self-assessment tests. I love self-assessment tests, for they help identify key traits, characteristics, skills, and simply more about a person. Below is a list of self-assessment tests and books I recommend for a person to learn more about themselves. I always say, the better you know yourself, the better leader/instructor you will be.

TIP: These are also excellent tests to have your students to take; for the more you know them, the easier it is to teach them.

FREE Self-Assessment Tests

- Learning Style—
  http://www.engr.ncsu.edu/learningstyles/
  ilsweb.html
- Brain Type—
  http://similarminds.com/brain.html
- Personality Type—
  http://www.personalitytype.com/
- DiSC (Dominant - Influence - Steady -
  Compliant)—
  http://www.123test.com/disc-personality-
  test/
- Values—
  http://www.mrs.umn.edu/services/career/c
  areer_planning/valquestion.php
- Emotional Intelligence—
  http://www.queendom.com/tests/access_p
  age/index.htm?idRegTest=1121
- Power—
  http://www.queendom.com/tests/access_p
  age/index.htm?idRegTest=1125
- Leadership Skills & Style Test—
  http://ww.queendom.com/tests/access_pa
  ge/index.htm?idRegTest=702
- Multiple Intelligence—
  http://www.businessballs.com/freemateri
  alsinex-
  cel/free_multiple_intelligences_test.xls
- Working Resources Self-Assessment Quiz-
  zes—

http://dwp.bigplanet.com/workingresourc
es/quicksurveys/

Books (I highly recommend these, each comes
with a code to take a self-assessment test)

- StrengthsFinder 2.0, Tom Rath—
  **http://www.strengthsfinder.com/home.as
  px**
    - Out of the 34 strengths theories, my
      top five are: (1) Responsibility, (2)
      Belief, (3) Activator, (4) Connected-
      ness, and (5) Positivity (see screen
      shot below).

Your Top Five Clifton StrengthsFinder Themes

Executing	Influencing	Relationship Building	Strategic Thinking
Responsibility	Activator	Connectedness	
Belief		Positivity	

- StandOut, Marcus Buckingham—
  http://standout.tmbc.com/gui/
    - Out of the nine roles, my top two
      are Connector and Teacher (see
      screen shot below)

YOUR STRENGTHS ROLES: RANK ORDER			
1	❂	CONNECTOR	You are a catalyst. Your power lies in your craving to put two things together to make something bigger than it is now.
2	🍎	TEACHER	You are thrilled by the potential you see in each person. Your power comes from learning how to unleash it.
3	☂	PROVIDER	You sense other people's feelings and you feel compelled to recognize these feelings, give them a voice and act on them.
4	✎	INFLUENCER	You engage people directly and convince them to act. Your power is your persuasion.
5	✐	CREATOR	You make sense of the world, pulling it apart, seeing a better configuration, and creating it
6	⚖	EQUALIZER	You are a level-headed person whose power comes from keeping the world in balance, ethically and practically
7	✦	ADVISOR	You are a practical, concrete thinker who is at your most powerful when reaching to and solving other people's problems.
8	✳	STIMULATOR	You use the host of other people's emotions. You feel responsible for them, for turning them around, for elevating them
9	♫	PIONEER	You see the world as a friendly place where, around every corner, good things will happen. Your distinctive power starts with your optimism in the face of uncertainty.

Therefore, what can I learn from all these tests and why take them? I take self-assessment tests each year to help me identify my changing skills, interests, and to validate my strengths and passions. I have used many of the statements from these self-assessment tests on my resume in the *Qualification* section. Why not? These tests state what I am good at, so I am going to use them for my benefit.

Additional Suggested Readings:

- *Brain Rules: 12 Principles for Surviving and Thriving at Work, Home, and School*, John Medina
- *Drive: The Surprising Truth About What Motivates Us*, Daniel H. Pink

- *Fascinate: Your 7 Triggers to Persuasion and Captivation*, Sally Hogshead
- *Go Put Your Strengths to Work: 6 Powerful Steps to Achieve Outstanding Performance*, Marcus Buckingham
- *How to Wow: Proven Strategies for Selling Your [Brilliant] Self in Any Situation*, Frances Cole Jones
- *Influencer: The Power to Change Anything*, Kerry Patterson, Joseph Grenny, David Maxfield, Ron McMillan, and Al Switzler
- *Moonwalking With Einstein: The Art and Science of Remembering Everything*, Joshua Foer
- *Off Balance: Getting Beyond the Work-Life Balance Myth to Personal and Professional Satisfaction*, Matthew Kelly
- *Presentation Zen: Simple Ideas on Presentation on Design and Delivery*, Garr Reynolds
- *Reaching Out: Interpersonal Effectiveness and Self-Actualization* (10th Edition), David H. Johnson
- *Soar With Your Strengths: A Simple Yet Revolutionary Philosophy of Business and Management*, Donald O. Clifton and Paula Nelson
- *Teach With Your Strengths: How Great Teachers Inspire Their Students*, Jo Ann Miller and Jennifer Robison

- *The Exceptional Presenter: A Proven Formula to Open Up and Own the Room*, Timothy J. Koegel
- *Wellbeing: The Five Essential Elements*, Tom Rath and James K. Harter, Ph.D.

Be a Life Learner

I am not a teacher, but an awakener.
—Robert Frost

Image Credit - 123RF

A teacher of any type must be a life learner, or in other words, someone who consistently learns through reading, researching, taking courses, and teaching courses. In my opinion, there is nothing worse than having a teacher who has not kept up his/her learning in their specific discipline of teaching.

For example, I teach many different technology courses, and I would be a poor teacher if I did not stay current with my technology skills. Microsoft Office's latest version is 2010, but if I told my students I only know 2003, I would lose credibility because I was so far behind in the latest technology. I currently run Microsoft Office 2003, 2007, and 2010 on my computer in my office. I do not say this to impress you, but to demonstrate that it is a requirement for just one of the schools, where I am an adjunct instructor.

An adjunct instructor can stay current in his/her discipline through additional readings on the discipline via trade journals, the Internet (RSS Feeds, blogs, social media), certifications, professional memberships, and/or even obtaining a higher degree or another degree.

Using the School's Development Tools

The mind is not a vessel to be filled,
but a fire to be kindled.
—Plutarch

Image Credit: 123RF

When you are hired by a school, many of them have great faculty development programs for its entire faculty, including adjunct instructors. Therefore, take advantage of the school's faculty development opportunities. Additionally, some schools encourage its faculty, including adjunct instructors, to create and deliver professional development workshops. This is a great resume builder for the adjunct instructor.

Developing Yourself

It does not matter how slowly you go as long as you do not stop.
—Confucius

Image Credit: 123RF

One of the most common phrases I have heard from other adjunct instructors is: *"I don't have time to learn or develop myself."* The truth is *you do.* Just as we expect our students to do their homework on time, so must an adjunct instructor take the time to learn and stay current in his/her discipline. The Internet is an adjunct instructor's best friend when it comes to self-development.

Several sites provide FREE training of all kinds (e.g., software programs, discipline specific programs, and more). Below is just a small list of ways to develop yourself.

Free Courses

- Coursera—As the website states, "The World's Best Courses. Online, for Free." https://www.coursera.org/
- 500 Free Online Courses from Top Universities—http://www.openculture.com/freeonlinecourses
- 200 Free Online Classes to Learn Anything—http://oedb.org/library/beginning-online-learning/200-free-online-classes-to-learn-anything/
- About U—http://u.about.com/
- AcademicEarth—http://www.academicearth.org/
- Berkley Webcasts—http://webcast.berkeley.edu/
- Computer Training, Education, & Tutorial Resources in IT—http://intelligentedu.com/
- Ed2Go—http://www.ed2go.com/
- EduFire—http://edufire.com/
- Education Online For Computers—http://educationonlineforcomputers.com/
- eLearning Course Center—http://www.e-learningcenter.com/free.htm
- Free Education Network—http://free-ed.net/free-ed/FreeEdMain01.asp
- Free Online Courses and Certification—http://alison.com/
- Free Online Courses and Education—http://education-por-

tal.com/article_directory/Free_Online_Cours
es_and_Education.html

- GCF Learn Free—
  http://www.gcflearnfree.org/
- Harvard Open Courses—
  http://www.extension.harvard.edu/open-learning-initiative
- LearnOutLoud—
  http://www.learnoutloud.com/
- LearnThat—**http://learnthat.com/**
- LearnTheNet—
  http://www.learnthenet.com/index.php
- MIT Open Courseware—
  http://ocw.mit.edu/index.htm
- Stanford's Free Online Courses—
  http://www.stanford.edu/online/courses
- The American Distance Education Consorti-
  um—**http://adec.edu/**
- Udacity—The website states, "You learn by
  solving challenging problems and pursuing
  udacious projects with world-renowned university instructors (not by watching long, bor-
  ing lectures)." **http://www.udacity.com/**
- Universities With Best Free Online Courses—
  **http://education-por-
  tal.com/articles/Universities_with_the_Best_Free
  _Online_Courses.html**
- US San Diego—**http://podcast.ucsd.edu/**
- Yale Open Courses—**http://oyc.yale.edu/**

Free Courses and Book Reviews

- Harvard Mentor Manager—This is a great way to take courses from Harvard instructors at a fraction of the cost. **http://hbr.org/harvardmanagementor?referral =01121**
- Soundview Executive Book Summaries— **http://www.summary.com/**
- GetAbstract—**http://www.getabstract.com/**
- Business Book Summaries— **http://www.bizsum.com/**
- AudioTech— **http://www.audiotech.com/business-summaries/**

Industry Reviews

(the below list is Business specific)

- Harvard Business Publishing for Educators— **http://hbsp.harvard.edu/**
- Harvard Business Review Magazine— **http://hbr.org/**
- Harvard Business School Working Knowledge—**http://hbswk.hbs.edu/**
- McKinsey Quarterly— **http://www.mckinseyquarterly.com/home.as px**
- MIT Sloan Management Review— **http://sloanreview.mit.edu/**
- Wharton University of Pennsylvania— **http://knowledge.wharton.upenn.edu/**

Free eBooks and Audio Books
- Audible—**http://www.audible.com/**
- Books Should Be Free—**http://www.booksshouldbefree.com/**
- We Give Books—**http://www.wegivebooks.org/?gclid=CJLcz9a PmrMCFfBcMgod9wQAlg**
- Project Gutenberg—**http://www.gutenberg.org/**
- Read Central—**http://readcentral.com/**
- Free e-Books—**http://www.free-ebooks.net/**
- Many Books—**http://manybooks.net/**
- 20 Best Websites to Download Free eBooks—**http://www.hongkiat.com/blog/20-best-websites-to-download-free-e-books/**

Learn a Language
- The Pimsleur Approach—**http://www.pimsleurapproach.com/**
- Babbel—**http://www.babbel.com/**
- BBC Languages—**http://www.bbc.co.uk/languages/**
- LiveMocha—**http://livemocha.com/**
- BabelFish—**http://www.babelfish.com/**
- Rosetta Stone—**http://www.rosettastone.com**
- Fluenz—**http://www.fluenz.com**
- Learn A Language—**http://www.learnalanguage.com/**

Social Networks and Additional Teaching Opportunities via the Internet

- Udemy—**http://www.udemy.com/**
- Connexions—**http://cnx.org/**
- Sclipo—**http://sclipo.com/**
- Skillshare—**http://www.skillshare.com/**
- We Teach Me—**http://weteachme.com/**
- Event Brite—**http://www.eventbrite.com**
- ed2go—**http://www.ed2go.com/TeachWithUs.aspx**
- Teach Writing Online—**http://www.writing-world.com/freelance/teach.shtml**

TIP: To get you excited about teaching online for yourself, check out this blog posting: *A new way to make six figures on the web—teaching*: **http://gigaom.com/2012/05/17/a-new-way-to-make-six-figures-on-the-web-teaching/**

Technology
and the Adjunct Instructor

Education is not the filling of a pail,
but the lighting of a fire.
—W.B. Yeats

Image Credit: 123RF

In today's adjunct industry, it is important that you have technical proficiencies in several areas — not just, I can play on **Facebook**, and can check my email; but really be able to maneuver several different technologies.

For example, one of the universities that I am an adjunct for requires me to know the following technologies:

Course Administration
- The school's faculty portal (central place for all the other technologies)

- The grade/attendance system
- Web mail
- The HR system
- The professional development system
- Campus webinars for training
- The campus laptop, copiers, and printers

Online Course Room Administration
- Learning management system
- The eText system
- The online library
- The Internet
- Microsoft Word, Excel, PowerPoint, and some cases Access

Classroom Administration
- Classroom personal computer
- Adding a laptop to the classroom technology
- Overhead projector
- DVD player
- VHS player
- Document Camera
- The campus computer lab

Additional Technologies That Could be Used in a Classroom
- Presentation software (Prezi, Knovio, etc.)
- Skype or Adobe Connect for streaming in guest lecturers

- Social Media
- The Internet and different search engines
- Wikis, Blogs, and Podcasts
- The list goes on and is only limited by the instructor's imagination. Please remember, technology is an enhancer to the learning, not a replacement.
- One of my favorite people to follow is Jane Hart. She has her top tech picks each day, and yearly she produces, "The Top 100 Tools for Learning" report. Here is her website: **Center for Learning & Performance Technologies**, **http://c4lpt.co.uk/**.

The above list equals approximately a dozen log-in names and passwords. This is just one of the schools I teach for, so increase the amount of technologies by the amount of schools I teach for and the type of teaching I do for each school (e.g., face-to-face, blended, online).

If you do not like technology, you will not like being an adjunct instructor—it is one of the main requirements of being an adjunct instructor in today's 21st-century classroom. I like to refer to myself as a Professor 2.0.

Social Media
and the Adjunct Instructor

Knowledge will bring you the opportunity
to make a difference.
—Claire Fagin

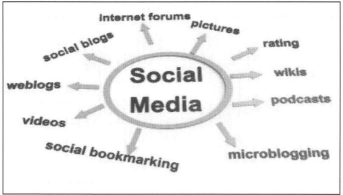

Image Credit: 123RF

I truly believe, without a shadow of doubt, that if you really want to become an adjunct instructor in today's competitive market, you MUST have a social media platform. Your social media presence could be very minimal (you have a **LinkedIn** account) or be a really impressive social media platform (you have **LinkedIn** profile, your own web page, your own blog, a **Twitter** page, a **Facebook** page, a **YouTube** channel, and maybe even a **Pinterest** board).

The use of social media to build your adjunct instructor brand is only limited by your imagination. Below are a few suggestions on the top social media tools (**LinkedIn, Facebook**, and **Twitter**) that could help you build your adjunct instructor platform. (Reminder: these are just the top tools, there are so many social media channels you could use. To see the many social media channels that exist, check out, "*The Conversation Prism*" of Social Media, by visiting the following website: **http://www.theconversationprism.com/media/images/convoprism-poster-lg.jpg**. This graphic was created by Brian Solis and JESS3, and really shows all the channels of social media.)

Image Credit: 123RF

LinkedIn—Founded in 2002 and official launched on May 5, 2003. It is the world's largest professional networking site with more than 175 million members representing over 200 countries. To learn about **LinkedIn** and its impressive history, check out the following website:
 http://press.linkedin.com/about.

In my opinion, having a **LinkedIn** account is the most important piece of social media you need to begin with when you are starting to build your Adjunct Instructor Platform. I say this because it allows you to build more than a resume or curriculum vitae, but a global presence.

I find the following features perfect for highlighting you—the future Adjunct Instructor:

- **Personal Profile**—One of my favorite sections in this is "Summary of Experience" a great place to show-off what you can and have done
- **Professional Headline**—critical keywords that describe who you are, the first thing someone reads
- **Skills & Expertise**—this is great for listing key skills and expertise
- **Recommendations**—I like this area too, for I can seek recommendations on the positions I have held or holding and people can see immediately what type of teacher I am
- **Endorsements**—this is the new feature that gives quick kudos on my skills and expertise
- **Groups**—as stated earlier, LinkedIn has 115 groups for the keyword Adjuncts, 490 for the keyword Instructor, and 1,119 for the keyword Teacher—Opportunities, Opportunities

- **Answers**—a great area where you can ask and answer questions and become an expert in your field
- **Applications**—there are many great applications that you can link to your **LinkedIn** account: **Twitter**, **Slideshare**, and **WordPress** blog, just to name a few

Suggested LinkedIn Reading:

1. Maximizing LinkedIn for Sales and Social Media Marketing: An Unofficial, Practical Guide to Selling & Developing B2B Business on LinkedIn by Neal Schaffer
2. Windmill Networking: Understanding, Leveraging & Maximizing LinkedIn: An Unofficial, Step-by-Step Guide to Creating & Implementing Your LinkedIn Brand - Social Networking in a Web 2.0 World by Neal Schaffer
3. Rock the World with your Online Presence: Your Ticket to a Multi-Platinum LinkedIn Profile 2nd Edition by Lori Ruff
4. The Power Formula for LinkedIn Success: Kick-start Your Business, Brand, and Job Search by Wayne Breitbarth
5. I'm on LinkedIn—Now What? (Third Edition): A Guide to Getting the Most Out of LinkedIn by Jason Alba

6. 100+ Ways to Use **LinkedIn—
http://linkedintelligence.com/smart-ways-
to-use-linkedin/**

Image Credit: 123RF

Facebook—Founded in 2004 and has reached 1-Billion users. **Facebook** began as a personal sharing network; but evolved into both a personal and professional place for sharing data of all types, e.g., updates, photos, videos, and more. The best piece of advice I can provide in regards to **Facebook** is create two pages, a private page (family/friends only), and a public page (professional). I recommend this for you never know what your family and friends may post on your personal page, so do not take the risk with just a personal page; create a private page too.

The following is a list of suggested items to build your **Facebook** professional page.

- **Facebook Username for Page**—this is important to obtain the most professional user name for your **Facebook** fan (professional) page. The recommended is to obtain your own name.

- **Facebook Timeline**—this feature allows you to create a literal timeline of your life—personal or professional
- **About**—this section allows you to talk about who you are
- **Share Links**—post your favorite social media links (i.e., **LinkedIn**, **Twitter**, etc.)
- **Likes**—post the pages you like individuals, companies, and schools you want to teach for
- **Apps**—You can do many things with **Facebook** apps (bookmarks for quick re-engagement, social channels, newsfeeds, etc.)

Suggested Facebook Reading:

- **Facebook**—Facebook pages—**http://www.facebook.com/about/pages**
- Likeable Social Media: How to Delight Your Customers, Create an Irresistible Brand, and Be Generally Amazing on Facebook (And Other Social Networks) by Dave Kerpen
- How To Facebook—The No Nonsense Guide To Using Facebook by Dave Barry
- Facebook Marketing: An Hour a Day by Chris Treadaway and Mari Smith
- **Facebook Marketing All-in-One For Dummies**, by Amy Porterfield, Phyllis Khare, and Andrea Vahl

Twitter: Founded in 2006 by Jack Dorsey and is known as a microblogging service. This means, you can only send a short message or "tweet," as it is known, with 140 characters in the message. It is great for sharing top headlines, news stories, tips, etc. It is a real-time information-sharing network. There are over 500 million active users globally sharing information 140 characters at a time.

The following is a list of suggested items to build your **Twitter** page.

- **Create your Twitter Account**
    - **Tip:** If this is for your platform, then use your whole name. For example, mine is @MichellePost (the "@" symbol denotes that this is my Twitter ID)
    - If this is for your business, use your whole business name if possible, sometimes that name may be taken.
- **Add your professional photo.**
    - **Tip:** The photo you use here needs to be the same photo on your LinkedIn profiles and your Face-

book public page. One of the main rules of social media is ensuring that all the pieces are consistent in color schemes, fonts, naming, professional photo, and email address.

- **Create your Bio box**—This area gives you 160 characters to tell your "story," so make it count. This short bio is what others will see when they bring up your profile, so you want it to be "powerful" and "informative" at the same time.
- **Begin Following others**—Follow people, companies, and organizations, all of which are influencers.

Suggested Twitter Reading:

- Take the Twitter Tour: **http://support.twitter.com/groups/31-twitter-basics/topics/182-announcements-and-new-stuff/articles/20169519-twitter-tour-let-us-show-you-around#**
- Twitter 101: How should I get started using Twitter?— http://support.twitter.com/groups/31-twitter-basics/topics/104-welcome-to-twitter-support/articles/215585-twitter-101-how-should-i-get-started-using-twitter#
- *The Twitter Book* by Tim O'Reilly and Sarah Milstein

- *Twitter Power 2.0: How to Dominate Your Market One Tweet at a Time* by Joel Comm and Anthony Robbins
- *The Tao of Twitter: Changing Your Life and Business 140 Characters at a Time* by Mark Schaefer

Final Words

Good luck and have fun, Building Your Adjunct Instructor Platform!

Follow me on **Twitter (@MichellePost)** for daily Adjunct Tips, Adjunct Opportunities, and Technology in Education tips.

Thanks for reading and please leave a review on Amazon of what you liked, what I can improve, and what other information you would like to learn.

Resources

Adjunct Instructor Job Sites

- Academic360: http://www.academic360.com/
- Academic Careers: http://www.academiccareers.com/
- Adjunct Instructor Jobs: http://www.adjunctInstructorjobs.com/
- Adjunct Jobs: http://adjunctjob.com/
- Adjunct Nation: http://www.adjunctnation.com/jobs/
- Adjunct Professor Jobs: http://www.adjunctprofessorjobs.com/
- Adjunctopia: http://adjunctopia.com/
- Education Job Site: http://www.educationjobsite.com/
- HigherEdJobs: http://www.higheredjobs.com/
- Indeed: http://www.indeed.com/q-Adjunct-Faculty-jobs.html
- Simply Hired: http://www.simplyhired.com/a/jobs/list/q-adjunct+faculty

Adjunct Instructor Online Job Sites

- Adjunct Instructor Online: http://www.adjunctInstructoronline.com/

- Adjunct Professor Online:
  http://www.adjunctprofessoronline.com/
- Online Instructional Jobs:
  http://home.surewest.net/tcsmith/oi-jobs.htm
- Online Teaching Jobs:
  http://onlineteachingjoblist.blogspot.com/
- Online Adjunct Faculty Position:
  http://onlineadjunctfacultyposition.com/
- Online Adjunct Jobs:
  http://onlineadjunctjobs.blogspot.com/

Using Job Search Engines

Use Keywords "Adjunct Faculty," "Adjunct Instructor," and / or "Adjunct Professor"

- Career Builder:
  http://www.careerbuilder.com/
- Dice: http://www.dice.com/
- Indeed: http://www.indeed.com/
  - Example:
    http://www.indeed.com/q-Adjunct-Instructor-jobs.html
- Glassdoor:
  http://www.glassdoor.com/index.htm
  - Example:
    http://www.glassdoor.com/Job/adjunct-instructor-jobs-SRCH_KO0,18.htm

- Jobster: **http://www.jobster.com/**
- The Ladders: **http://www.theladders.com/**
- Monster: **http://www.monster.com/**
    - Example: **http://jobsearch.monster.com/searc h/__22adjunct-instructor__22_5**
- Salary: **http://salary.com/**
    - Example: **http://swz.salary.com/salarywizard/ layout- scripts/swzl_selectjob.aspx?txtKey word=adjunct+instructor&txtZipC ode=**
- Simply Hired: **http://www.simplyhired.com/**
    - Example: **http://www.simplyhired.com/a/job s/list/q-adjunct+instructor**

TIP: The **bit.ly** program for shortening web addresses (URLs) was used to make the full web addresses from the searches more manageable.

Adjunct Job Specific Sites

- Academic360: **http://www.academic360.com/**
- Academic Careers Online: **http://www.academiccareers.com/**

- Academic Employment Network: http://www.academploy.com/
- Adjunct Professor Jobs: http://www.adjunctprofessorjobs.net/
- Chronicle of Higher Education: http://chronicle.com/section/Home/5
- Education America: http://www.educationamerica.net/
- Education Jobs: http://www.educationjobs.com/
- EdJoin: http://www.edjoin.org/
- HigherEd Jobs: http://www.higheredjobs.com/
- HowToTeachOnline: http://www.howtoteachonline.com/online-teaching-jobs/
- Job-Hunt: http://www.job-hunt.org/
- Jobs PhDs: http://www.jobs.phds.org/
- Online Adjunct Jobs: http://www.onlineadjunctjobs.blogspot.com/
- PhDs: http://www.phds.org/
- PostDocJobs: http://www.postdocjobs.com/
- ScholaryHires: http://scholarlyhires.com/
- Teacher Jobs: http://www.teacherjobs.com/
- Teaching-Jobs: http://www.teaching-jobs.org/

- Teachers-Teachers: **http://www.teachers-teachers.com/**
- Top Higher Education Jobs: **http://www.tedjob.com/**
- University Jobs: **http://www.universityjobs.com/**

LinkedIn Groups For Adjunct Instructors

TIP: Log into your LinkedIn account, select Groups, and then do a keyword search for "adjunct." LinkedIn currently has 113 groups that have the word "adjunct" in its group name. However, there are other groups for teachers, instructors, and educators. Below is only a small listing of some of the groups with the largest amount of members.

- **Online Faculty-Adjunct, Full-Time, University Administrators**
- **The Adjunct Network**
- **Online Adjunct Professors**
- **Adjunct Faculty Directory**
- **Online Adjunct Rolodex**
- **Adjunct Instructors/Professors**
- **Adjunct Network Community Colleges**
- **HigherEdJobs**
- **Able Adjuncts**
- **Educator/Instructor Career Network**
- **New Faculty Majority**
- **Online Adjunct Instructors**
- **Online Instructors**

Sites for Online Adjunct Jobs and Online Schools

- Distance Education Reviews: http://www.distance-education.org/Reviews/
- Distance Education Schools: http://www.distance-education.org/Schools/
- Distance Learning College Guide: http://www.distance-learning-college-guide.com/
- Earn My Degree: http://www.earnmydegree.com/
- ELearners: http://www.elearners.com/
- GradSchools: http://www.gradschools.com/
- Guide to Online Education: http://www.guidetoonlineschools.com/
- Online Colleges: http://www.online-education.net/online-colleges/index.html
- Online Education Database: http://oedb.org/
- Petersons: http://www.petersons.com/
- Universities: http://www.universities.com/
- WorldWide Learn: http://www.worldwidelearn.com/

Adjunct Instructors Resources

- Academic Keys:
  http://www.academickeys.com/
- Adjunct Nation:
  http://www.adjunctnation.com/
- Education World:
  http://www.educationworld.com/
- eLearners: **http://www.elearners.com/**
- Faculty Finder:
  http://www.facultyfinder.com/
- The Chronicle:
  http://chronicle.com/section/Home/5
- IMCA Resources:
  http://bookstore.icma.org/Resources_for_I nstructors_W9.cfm
- World Wide Learn:
  http://www.worldwidelearn.com/

Articles, Blogs, eBooks, Books, and Videos

Articles

- ScholaryHires.com has a great listing of articles on its site:
  http://www.scholarlyhires.com/Applicant /Articles/All-Applicant-Advice-Journals

- I want to Become an Adjunct Professor - **http://aunicereed.hubpages.com/hub/I-Want-to-Become-an-Adjunct-Professor**
- Go Teach a Course!— **http://icma.org/en/icma/career_network/education/teaching_resources/go_teach**
- How to Become an Online Adjunct Professor - **http://www.adjunctprofessoronline.com/content/how-to-become-an-online-adjunct-professor-0**
- How to Become Online Adjunct Teacher - **http://education-por-tal.com/articles/How_to_Become_an_Online_Adjunct_Teacher.html**

Blogs

- Dr. K.T. Erwin: **http://www.squidoo.com/onlineteachingjobs**
- eHow Contributor: **How to Become an Adjunct Instructor**
- Jacqueline Chinappi: **Getting an Online Adjunct Faculty Position**
- Jared Lewis blog posting: **How to Obtain the Qualifications of an Adjunct Instructor**

- Mary Wroblewski: **How to Apply to Be an Adjunct Instructor**
- Online Teaching Makes Money: **http://onlineteachingmakesmoney.com/**

eBooks

- Schools That Hire Online Adjunct Faculty: An Updated Database for Online Instructors, Nicolas Veracruz (Amazon Kindle)
- How to Find Online Teaching Employment Opportunities and Landing a Teaching Job Online: **http://www.online-teaching-employment.com/Welcome.html**
- The following Google search provides several Adjunct Faculty Handbooks for your viewing pleasure to see what schools are requiring—**http://bit.ly/NcgW23**

Books

(Getting Hired as an Adjunct)

- *5 Secrets for Finding an Online Teaching Jobs*, Brian Robison
- *Become an Academic Free Agent*, Michael Finney
- *Get Hired to Teach Online*, Amy Peterson
- *How To Make Money Teaching Online*, Michael Peterson

- *How to Teach Online Without Selling Your Soul: Build Your Own e-Learning Business, Create Unique Content And Work From Anywhere*, André Klein
- *Inside Secrets of Finding a Teaching Job*, Jack Warner, Clyde Bryan, and Diane Warren
- *I Want a Teaching Job . . .*, Tim Wei
- *Land Your First Online Teaching Job*, Jean E. Sibley
- *Make Money Teaching Online*, Danielle Babb and Jim Mirabella
- *Online Teaching Secrets Revealed*! Jaime Vendera
- *Road to Teaching . . .*, Eric Hougan
- *Schools That Hire Online Adjunct Faculty . . .*, Nicolas Veracruz
- *Teacher Interviews: How to Get Them and How to Get Hired!*, Robert W. Pollock
- *Teach Online: 10 Simple Steps to get Your Resume Noticed and Land the Job*, Dr. Carolyn Edwards
- *Teach Online! A Practical Guide for Finding Online Faculty Positions, Getting into The Distance Education Industry and Making Money from Home*, Dr. Marina Kostina
- *The Definitive Guide to Getting a Teaching Job . . .*, Mary C. Clement
- *The In's and Out's of Online Instruction Transitioning from Brick and Mortar to*

Online Teaching, Dr. Danan Myers-Wylie, Dr. Jackie Mangieri, Donna Hardy

(Teaching Tools)

- *Empowering Online Learning: 100+ Activities for Reading, Reflecting, Displaying, and Doing*, Curtis J. Bonk and Ke Zhang
- *Grading Made Fast and Easy*, Leslie Bowman
- *Managing Online Instructor Workload: Strategies for Finding Balance and Success*, Simone C.O. Conceicao and Rosemary M. Lehman
- *The Adjunct Faculty Handbook*, Lorrie E. Cooper and Bryan A. Booth
- *The Excellent Online Instructor: Strategies for Professional Development*, Rena M. Palloff and Keith Pratt
- *The New Professor's Handbook*, Bakari Akil II, Ph.D.
- *The Online Teaching Survival Guide: Simple and Practical Pedagogical Tips*, Judith V. Boettcher and Rita-Marie Conrad
- *The Teaching Assistants' Bible*, Bakari Akil II, Ph.D.
- *Tools for Teaching*, Barbara Gross Davis

(Teaching Philosophy)

- *Called to Teach*, William Yount
- *Teaching to Change Lives*, Howard Hendricks
- *Teach What You Know*, Steve Trautman
- *Teach With Your Strengths*, Rosanne Liesveld, Jo Ann Miller, and Jennifer Robison
- *The Courage to Teach*, Parker J. Palmer
- *The One Minute Teacher*, Constance Johnson
- *The Seven Laws of the Learner: How to Teach Almost Anything to Practically Anyone*, Bruce Wilkinson
- *The Skillful Teacher: Building Your Teaching Skills*, Jon Saphier, Mary Ann Haley-Speca, and Robert Gower

Future Books
for Adjunct Instructors

The Adjunctologist
The Adjunct Instructor and Technology —
The What, the Why and How of
Using Technology as an Adjunct Instructor

Social Media for Adjunct Instructors
Using Social Media to Help
Build Your Adjunct Instructor Platform & Teach
With It In The Classroom

eTools for Today's Professor 2.0
Tools to Help You Prepare, Present,
and be Productive as a Professor 2.0

ePublishing for the Adjunct Instructor
Learn to Share Your Expertise

The Adult Learner
Success Strategies for the Adjunct Instructor

References

Massy, M. (1990). *When values collide: Flashpoints*. Enterprise Media.

Massey, M. (2005). *What you are is where you were when, again!* Enterprise Media.

Ruben, H. E. (n.d.). *Adjunct Instructor definition*. Retrieved from **http://ezinearticles.com/?Adjunct-Instructor-Definition&id=2430104**

About the Author

ReachYourPotential:
http://reachyourpotential.info/
Twitter:
http://twitter.com/michellepost
LinkedIn:
http://www.linkedin.com/in/michellepostphd
Slideshare:
http://www.slideshare.net/mpostphd

Dr. Michelle Post has a broad career that spans more than 25 years in business and technology. She has been teaching in both corporate and now academia on a variety of subjects that include leadership, organizational development, human resource development, marketing, generation studies, social media, and technology in education.

Along with her expertise in leadership, management, and resource management, Dr. Post possesses strengths in client relations, systems engineering, business and network environments and technology integration, 20+ years of leadership and management experience. She also has a strong technical training background, with experience designing, administering, facilitating, and evaluating corporate training courses, training presentations, manuals, on-site, and distance learning environments.

Over the course of her career, Dr. Post has created and designed numerous training programs in leadership, professional development, technical skills and other areas, while developing employees for 25% productivity gains. She possesses exceptional communication skills, is experienced designing and delivering learning materials that convey complex concepts in clear terms, and is articulate in writing and in person.

Dr. Post is also noted for her energetic and demonstrative speaking skills, unorthodox ideas for solutions to problems and possessing a high level of behavioral versatility, providing the flexibility and responsiveness needed to handle a variety of situations or work environments.

Notes

33392846R00091

Made in the USA
San Bernardino, CA
22 April 2019